DESTINATION: A MORE CREATIVE YOU

“Creativity is contagious, pass it on.” – Albert Einstein

Fuel your Creativity

ANGELA CHAO
AND
SUSAN KSIEZOPOLSKI

Fuel Your Creativity

First Published in Mississauga in 2019 by My Words Press

ISBN 978-0-9916845-6-4

My Words Press

Designed and Edited by: Susan Ksiezopolski
Illustrated by: Angela Chao

Printed in Canada

Dedication

This book is dedicated to the artists of every genre and medium that inspire our journey in creating art; to budding new artists who have yet to discover and explore their talents, and to artists looking for motivation and/or new ways of practicing and enhancing their skills. Last but not least this book is especially for the artists that don't yet know they are artists and just happened on this book by chance.

May this book be the tool to fuel you towards your own creative journey to brilliance.

Preface

Poetry speaks softly, heard through the dialogue of inspiring words weaving stories. Through the rhythm and rhyme of verse on the page, the dialogue of self is heard. Narrative conveying experiences of the human condition are composed and shared shattering isolation, connecting us. Writing is the oxygen fuelling self-expression, unleashing the power to transform.

Art speaks in bold colours and vivid textures. Each brush stroke makes a statement, illustrating and liberating thoughts and feelings. Mindless doodles arise from the canvas, expressing emotions emerging from reflections within. Outpourings of images awaken wonder, silencing the mindless chatter as impressions surface and connect the art to meaning.

When poetry connects with art, it stretches and shifts self-expression to a new dimension. It creates a fresh artistic voice to communicate and to help translate the language of emotional literacy. The merging of poetry and art as a tool for creative expression is energizing and restorative. This is the intent of this book – that it be used as part of a reflective creative practice that uplifts and encourages further creativity empowering personal growth.

Cafes are breeding grounds, meeting places that can inspire creativity. History is rich of stories of young artists meeting in cafes, united by their common interest in creating, engaged in conversations about their lives, their world and how these are reflected in their body of work. Some examples of this are Vincent *van Gogh, Paul Gauguin, Pablo Picasso and Henri Matisse.*

It was at a meeting at Timothy's World Café in the Erin Mills Town Centre, Mississauga Canada that the seeds for *"Fuel Your Creativity"* were planted. It was the backdrop for the breeding ground that led to engaging discussions about the possibilities of how art and poetry could converge to create a new art form. The merger of abstract art with abstract poetry; creating an impactful fusion of art and poetry to reach and touch a broader audience was the concept behind Angela Chao, visual artist and Susan Ksiezopolski, poet, establishing *CreateConvergence.*

Combining poetry with art to communicate and connect, we fuel engaging exchanges that expand awareness and alter perceptions of our world and ourselves, creating the space for healing. This is the vision that brought Angela and Susan Ksiezopolski together to bring the *"Fuel Your Creativity" book to life.*

Introduction

Creatives often ponder and wonder about the approach related to inspiration. Where does it come from? How do we get more of it? Is it important and necessary to be inspired to create? Yet, the truth is that inspiration doesn't **come** to us. Rarely does it show up unannounced. In order for it to arrive, we must be active participants in the process, seek it and cultivate it. The more we take action to look to fill ourselves up with unique experiences and expose ourselves to a diverse variety of things, the more we will have to draw from – both literally and figuratively. Being inspired is a way of being in our world and how we live our life lays the foundation to bring forward inspiration.

Our wish for you, our fellow creatives, in creating this book is that it inspires you by helping to providing the backdrop, the space and the place for you to ponder and wonder. May it open pathways for your own creativity to flourish. The best way to set yourself up for success in being more creative is to follow the advice of another creative. In the words of Rumi *"The inspiration you seek is already within you. Be silent and listen."* Within each of us live the seeds for creativity. Inspiration comes from within. Allow yourself time and space to be with the pages in this book. Absorb the images and the words. Truly see and feel them speak to you. Listen for messages that resonate with you, awakening and touching a cord that needs to be expressed. Start from there.

Allow yourself to be present to the creative force waiting to express itself on the blank page. Don't judge as ideas stir, just allow the creativity to flow and see what magical, mystical and mysterious place it takes you. You might just be surprised where you find yourself.

There is no right or wrong way to be creative. Be open and flexible and approach each page with a sense of curiosity and wonder. Feel free to express yourself and fuel your creativity through the words and art on these pages.

Creativity promotes the discovery process. It can help us reconcile, restore, build, rectify, and regenerate. We can set ourselves up to overhaul our reality and move forward. Capturing our story on paper whether we do it through words or images relieves us of the burden of carrying our story hidden inside us. It lightens our load, diminishing the negative power the story has on us. This frees us to move forward with more confidence.

There is without a doubt a vibrant transformative energy that resonates within us and turns up the volume and colour of our lives when we are exposed to art in any form, be it music, literature or visual art. Art creates a bridge opening the space for conversations that create connections. This is why art has the power to uplift and motivate us. The imagination of other artists, poets, and musicians touches us. Through creative expression, we can see a part of ourselves we cannot give voice to. This helps us to validate our shared humanity. Art is how we make sense of our world and express who we are in it.

We might not be Mozart, Hemmingway or Picasso but sharing our creativity through the music we compose, the words we write and the art we create gives us the power to spark a flame of curiosity and wonder for others. What we create creates US. Immersing ourselves in all forms of art can provide us with a respite from our daily routines. We are transported into a place where we can float away inside a melody; give food for thought on some tough current world issues through cleverly crafted written stories, poetry/prose, or be distracted from it all as we blend with the colours and textures on a canvas, creating a visual vacation into delight.

Whether you are a musician, writer or artist, take some time to reflect and unleash your own creativity on the pages provided here.

You might find your creativity through words, music, art or meditation, don't stop looking and keep creating. When you allow yourself the time to be creative, it helps you to become more aware and fine-tunes you to hear the stories and messages in your life. Use this book to capture them in your preferred medium, be it visual, literary arts, or music. By capturing the experiences on canvas or on paper, we are better able to understand and make sense of our life experiences and enhance our sense of well-being. Creativity can help you metabolize your past or present in a way that brings greater liberation and joy – and we all deserve more of that.

Magic

Magic happens by chance
Not in anticipation
Magic happens by chance
Not on purpose
Magic happens by chance
Not with the wave of a wand
It happens when
We surrender to joy
With the abundance of possibilities
That can magically
Land in front of us
On our path
Unanticipated
Reconnecting us
To the magic
Already within us
Waiting for a chance
To come out

Susan Ksiezopolski

How to Use This Book

Whether you are a new writer or artist, just exploring your newfound interest or a serious enthusiast *Fuel Your Creativity* has been designed to enhance and support your creative practice. It is a place to come to and to be inspired. Just show up, open up to a page and open up to the creativity already waiting inside you to be released. Use these pages to reflect and write your own poetry and words or doodle your own art. Just like there is no right or wrong way to be creative there is no right or wrong way to use this book. As you move through this book, you can make your way systematically page by page, or you can randomly choose a page to engage with. Simply set an intention to be open to whatever comes up on the page for you to create. Go with the flow.

STEP ONE: Take a moment before you create, to get grounded. To do this experiment with different ways of moderating your breathing rhythm and trying out meditation techniques that help you get grounded and centred before you begin your creative process.

If you have a grounding practice for entering your creative zone than use that. If you don't have a practice or would like to experiment with new ways of setting the stage for being more focused and relaxed, try selecting a technique listed here, or search through the Internet for other practices that you may find more aligned with your interests and needs.

Breathing Techniques:

Abdominal Breathing also referred to as Deep Breathing:

With this technique you breathe from your belly. As you breathe in through your nose, your belly expands instead of your rib cage, as the air enters your lungs.
Take a deep breath, breathing in slowly through your nose. Feel the air filling your lungs as you expand your lower belly. Exhale through your mouth, by pushing the air out from the bottom of your lungs by contracting your diaphragm.
Repeat this three times.

4-7-8 Pattern Breathing:

Start on your out breath, by exhaling and emptying your lungs of air. Breathe in slowly and quietly through your nose for a count of 4. Hold your breath for a count of 7 and then exhale loudly through your mouth for a count of 8 making a blowing sound.
Repeat this three times

Equal Breathing:

With this technique your "out" breath and "in" breath will be of equal length. Inhale slowly and smoothly for 5 seconds and then slowly breathe out for 5 seconds. It's about creating a slow rhythmic pattern feeling the air move in through your nose and gently out through your mouth. The cycles should be natural and not forced. Do this for 5 – 10 minutes.

Breathing techniques can help to create a receptive relaxed state of mind that helps to clear the way to being more creative.

Meditation Techniques:

Progressive relaxation:

This is about systemically tensing and releasing muscle groups in your body. It is also referred to as body scanning, starting from toes and working your way up to your head. You can start by taking a few deep breaths and focusing on the areas of your body as you move through them. Tighten and contract the muscles as tight as you can, holding for a few seconds and then release as you progress slowly from your toes to your head. Start with your toes and move your way through your feet, calves, knees, thighs, legs, buttocks, lower back, middle back, upper back, hands, arms, shoulders, neck, jaw and your forehead.

Listen To Relaxing Music:

Listening to soft, instrumental, relaxing music is another way to enter a meditative reflective state. There are so many soundscape options to choose from. You may choose to have the music playing in the background as you create or listen to it before you start your creative process to awaken your muse. Search your own collection or here are some of our favourites: Dan Gibson Solitudes series; Tibetan Meditation music, Anthony Barr's Sacred Sevens flute music.

Visualization or Imagery Meditation:

This meditation engages your brain to help you relax and expanding your capacity for creativity. You start with closing your eyes and activating your imagination. Picture yourself in a comforting, calming place. A beach, a mountain, a forest or any scenery peaceful for you. Visualize yourself in that place and feel the landscape come alive activating your senses and bringing you into an increased state of responsiveness and mindfulness.

Walking Meditation

Walking meditation involves slow, mindfully walking in nature, taking in what you hear, see, feel, smell while you walk. It is a simple practice of bringing your mind into awareness as you move comfortably, pausing along the way to become present to your surroundings. The goal of this is to help you become calmer prepared to let your creativity flow more freely.

STEP TWO: Take a moment to focus and reflect on the page you have chosen. Look and focus on the art, the quote, the colours, and the image on that page. What speaks to you? What captures your attention? What comes to mind? How does it make you feel? How do the images and words spark your imagination? Use your reflections to inspire and fuel your creativity.

STEP THREE: Create. Write, draw or do both. Don't hold back, add colour, doodle. Just keep your pens/pencils moving, go with the flow. Allow it to fuel your creativity. Give yourself permission to be creative and to have fun.

“Nature is imagination itself” – William Blake

BLOOM

Summer flowers
Chased by Spring Showers
Bloom bright
Radiant light

The serenity of the beautiful summer sky
The freshness of the river in early spring
The colour on the leaves in autumn
The pattern of snowflakes in winter
All reminders of what life is like
Life is full of memories in these memories lives time
Life is the serenity of a summer sky
The coolness of the spring thaw
The brightness of the autumn colours
And the gentleness of the winter snowflakes

Summers Rain
36" x 48"
Acrylic on canvas

Summer Rain

Gentle rumbles roars
Across an electric sky
Breaking up the heat

Leaves tremble
In anticipation of
Cascading thunder

Flash of light
Cuts through gloom
As the downpour begins

Cloudburst reprieve
Scorching raindrops
Cut through the heat of day

Sizzling droplets
Captured by parched buds
Comforted by the rain
As it evaporates into the heat

“Creativity takes courage.” – Henri Matisse

bREATHE

HAVING MY PAST
HAVING MY PRESENT
HAVING MY FUTURE
TOGETHER IN ONE ROOM

IS AN OVERWHELMING FEELING

OUR TIMELESS FRIENDSHIP
BRINGS OUT
THE BEST PART OF ME

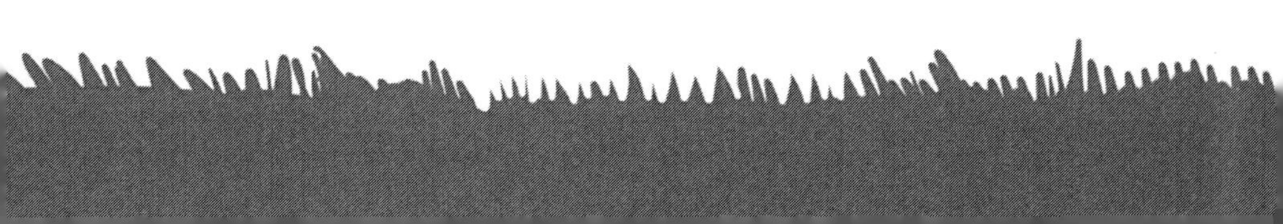

Within every breath
A MIRACLE
WAITS TO BE
released

“You can’t use your creativity, the more you use the more you have.” – Maya Angelou

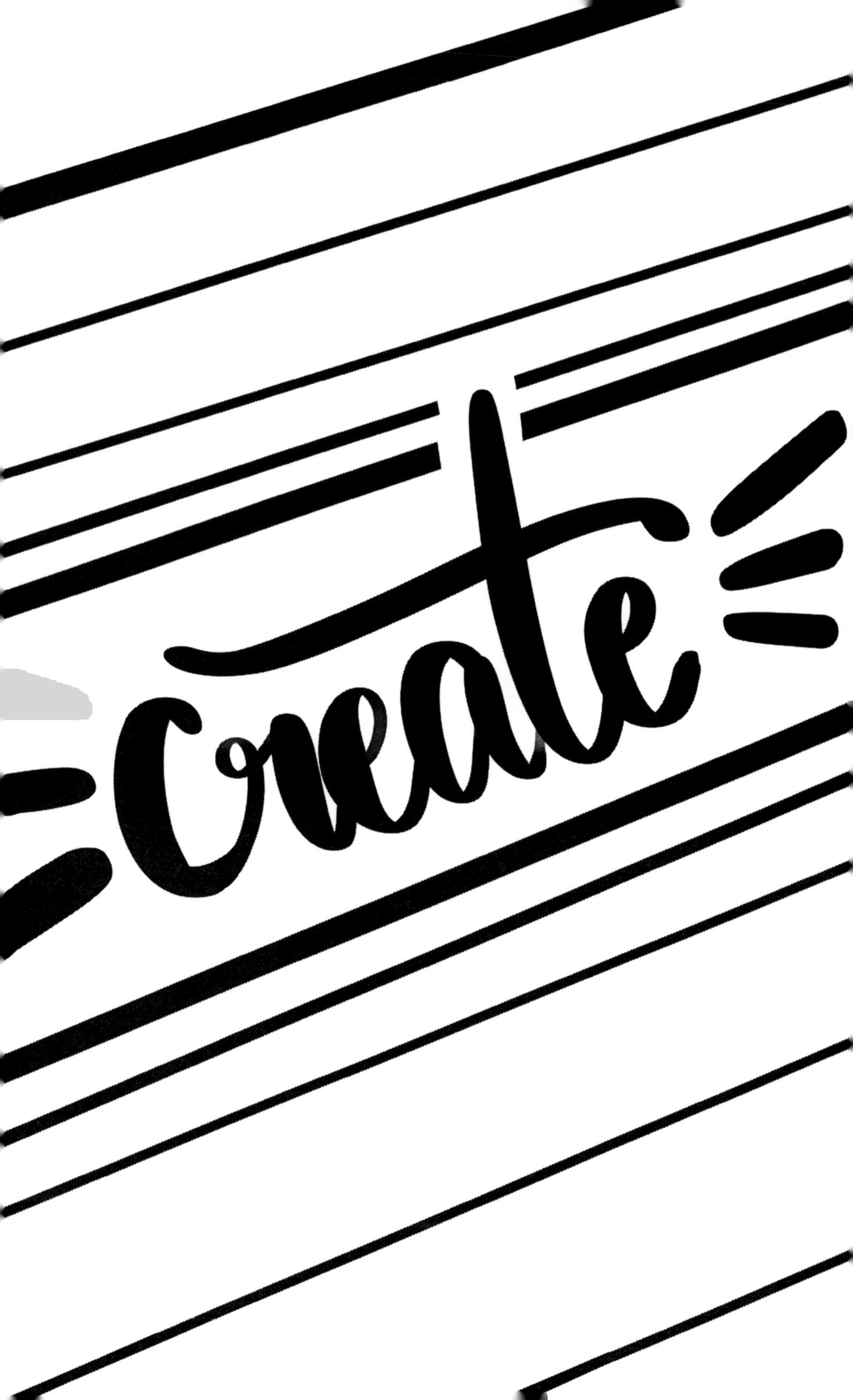
create

TANGLED UP
BURIED DEEP
BEHIND THE THOUGHTS
LOST
NOT EVEN ABLE TO
PEAK OUT

WE CREATIVES
ARTIST
MUSICIANS
ALL STORYTELLERS
WE USE OUR ART
TO HEAL OUR STORIES

OUTPOURING THE PAIN
CLEANSE NOT ONLY OURSELVES
REACHING OUT FROM
CANVAS COLORS
MUSIC MELODIES
WORDS WHISPERED

CLEANSE THE HEART
OF THOSE THAT SEE
AND TOUCH THE SAME STORY
INSIDE THEMSELVES
CREATING A LIFELINE TO
FREEDOM

“Creativity itself doesn't care at all about results, the only thing it craves is the process. Learn to love the process and let whatever happens next happen." - Elizabeth Gilbert

DISCOVER

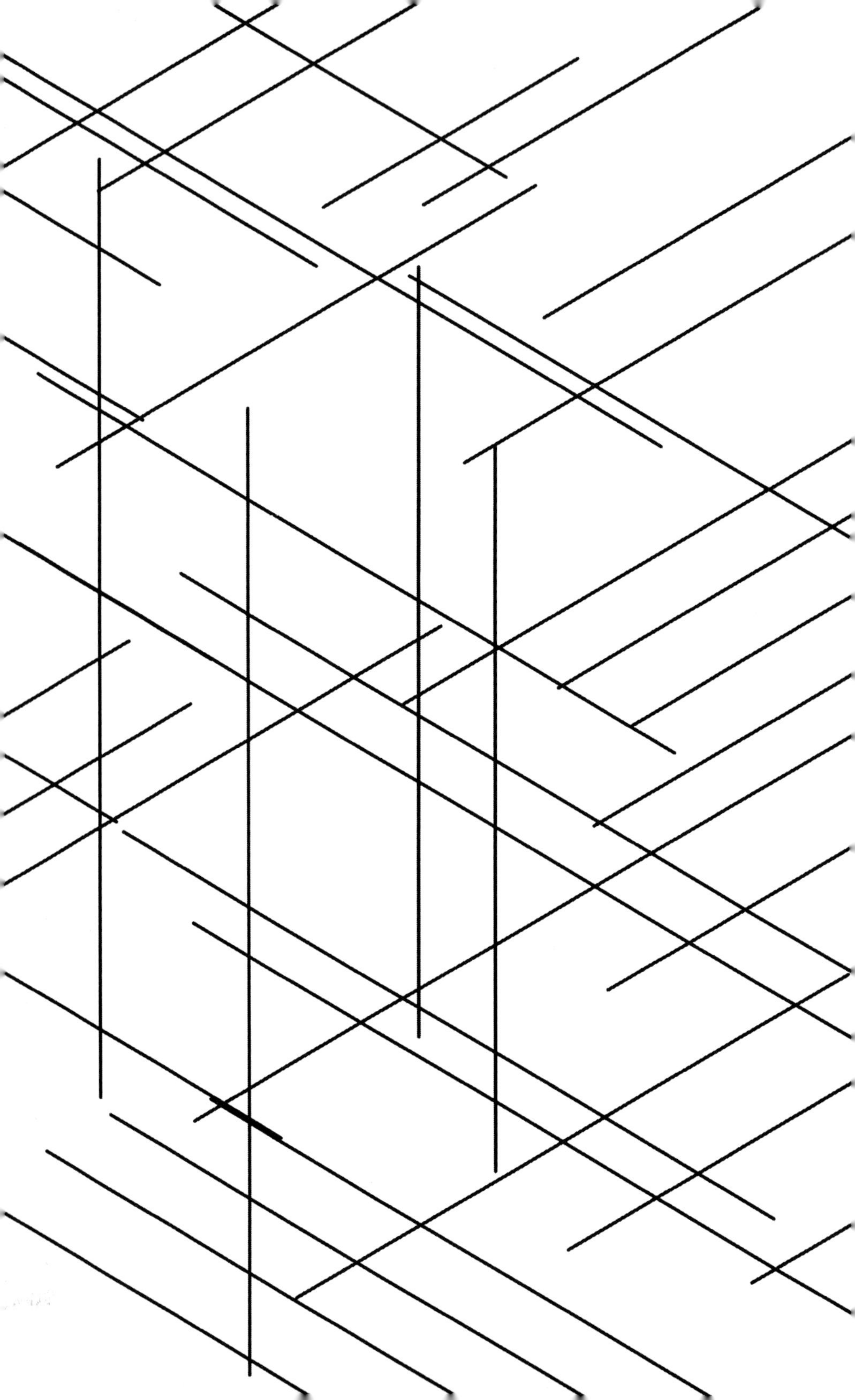

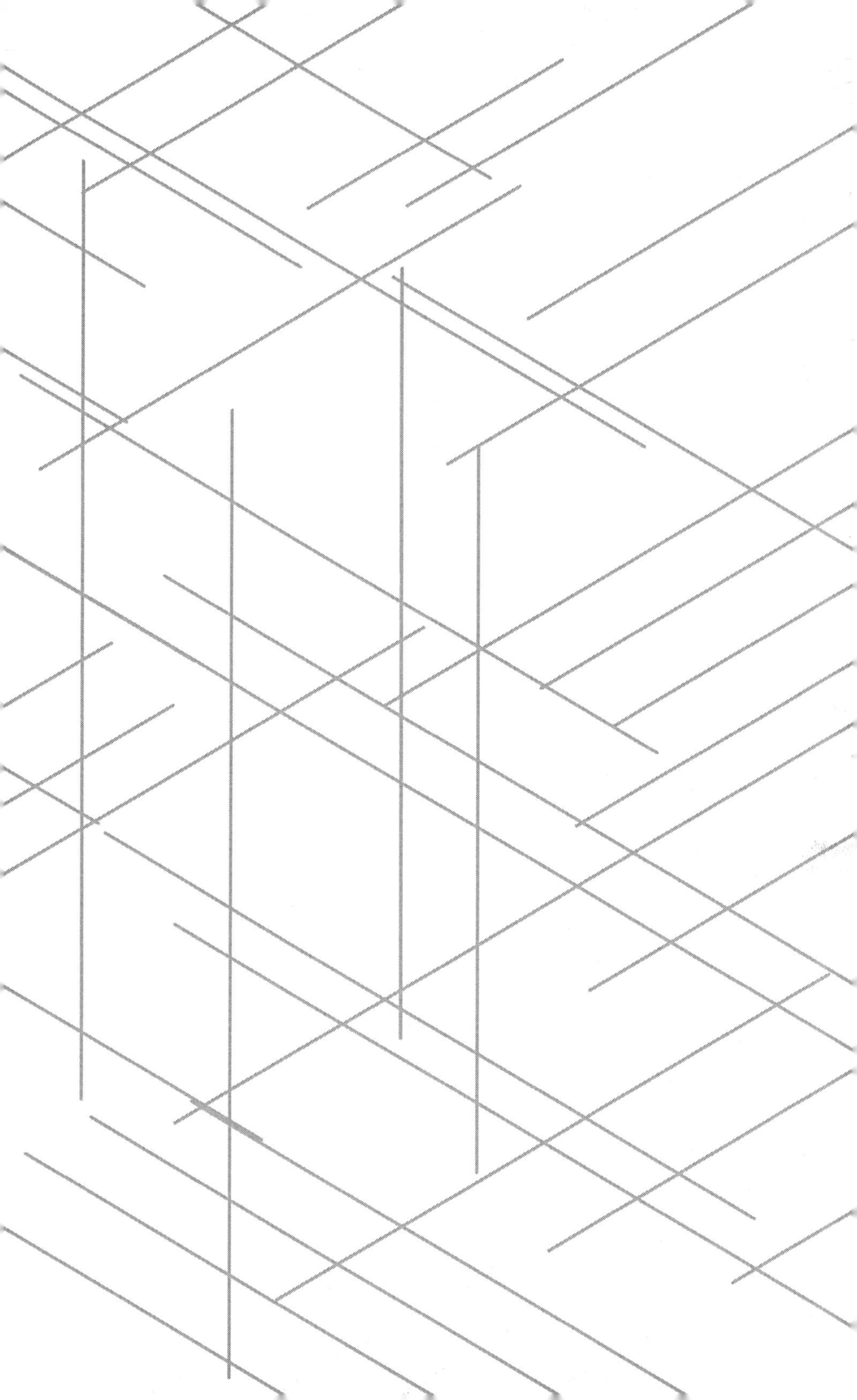

In the climb
Growing steadily
Reaching for the sunlight
Clinging to expand upwards

In the climb
Yearning to touch the stars
Intertwined and connected

In the climb
The purple radiance
Adds grace and a splash of colour
Peeking out between the backdrop
Giving thanks for the support
In the climb

ROAD AHEAD

WAITS FOR YOU TO BEGIN

BOLDLY LISTENING

TO THE SOUND

OF YOUR OWN HEART

BRAVELY LEADING YOU

BEYOND THE OPEN ROAD

ACROSS THE FINISH LINE

“I see your life as already artful, just waiting and ready for you to make it art.” – Toni Morrison

DREAM

CAN'T HEAR TRUTH
WHILE WE ARE
IN THE NOISE
OF OUR LIVES

The Beauty you see in my eyes is merely a reflection of the love in your eyes & within my heart

We think it is complicated
But the reality is
Your reason for
being Is simple

It
Is
What is

" I have nature and art and poetry and if that is not enough, what is enough?" – Vincent van Gogh

grow

RAINDROPS
LIKE SILKY DEW
CLING TO THE VELVET PETAL

PETALS
CATCH THE SUN
FLICKERING LIKE FIRE
SHINING BRIGHT
CONTRASTING
AGAINST THE GREEN BUD

BUDS
THAT HAVE YET
TO UNFOLD
AND WAIT PATIENTLY
FOR THEIR TURN TO SHINE

tears
are
words
of the
heart

HARDWIRED TO FRAZZLE
REPROGRAM TO DAZZLE
SOFT REBOOT IS REQUIRED

CLOSE ALL OPEN FILES
RESTART, REFRESH
ALLOW THE UNNEEDED TO VANISH

UNPLUG TO RELEASE
TAP INTO THE UN-RUFFLING
POWER OF STILLNESS

TANGLED WEBS DISAPPEAR
INTERNAL CONNECTIVITY IS RESTORED
BRIGHTNESS SETTING
SHIMMERING LIKE THE SUN

" The creative process is a process of surrender, not control."
– Julia Cameron

Healing

Truth
SPEAKS
Sliently
To us

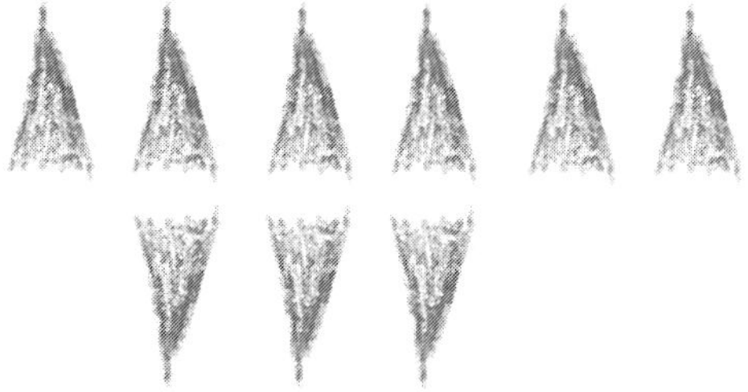

IN
TAKING
care of
OTHERS
you can
HEAL
yourself

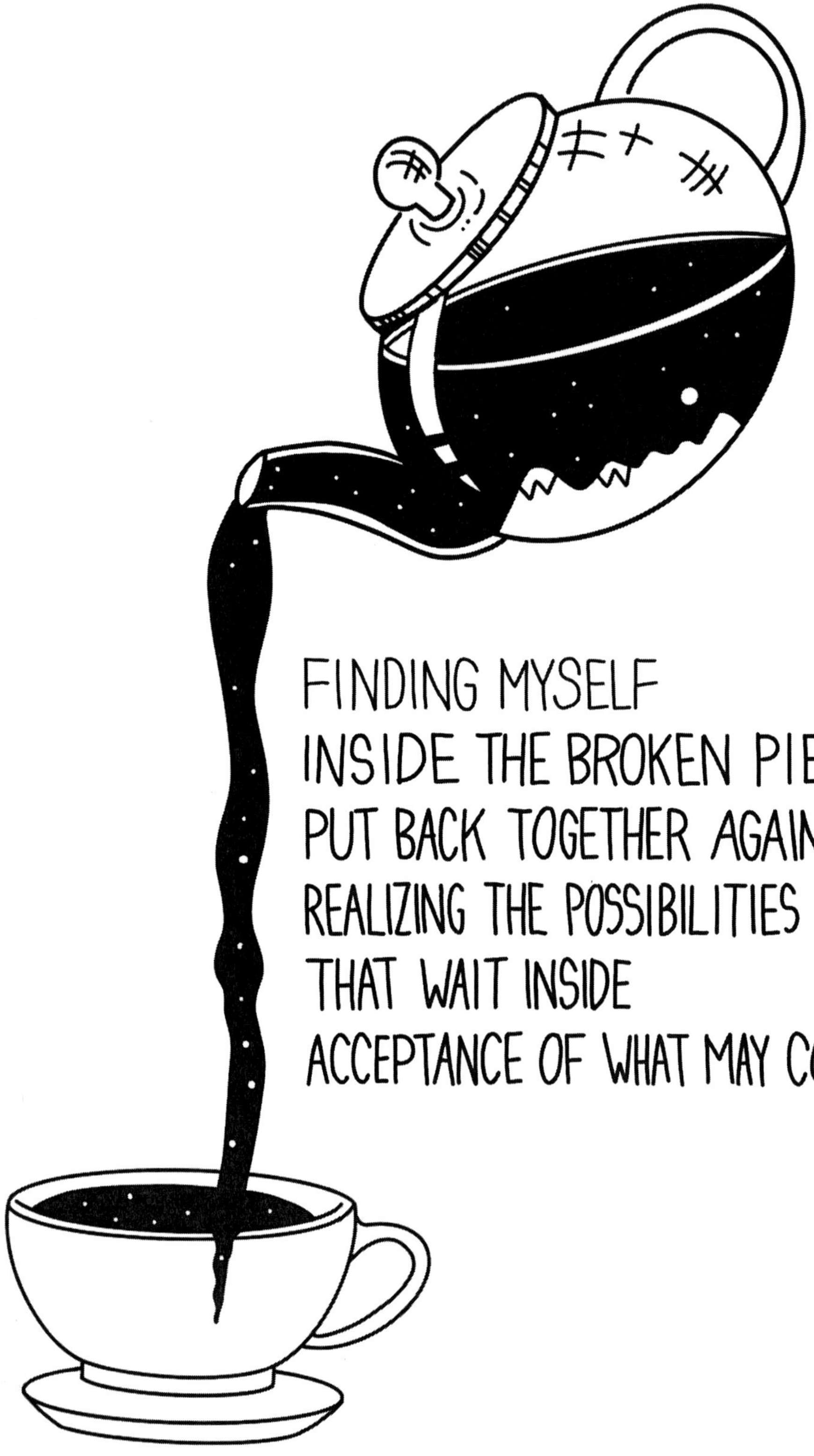

FINDING MYSELF
INSIDE THE BROKEN PIECES
PUT BACK TOGETHER AGAIN
REALIZING THE POSSIBILITIES
THAT WAIT INSIDE
ACCEPTANCE OF WHAT MAY COME

" The best and only thing that an artist can do for another is to serve as an example and an inspiration."

– Steven Pressfield

INSPIRE

the ancients
HOLDING TRADITION
passing down
THE TORCH

IN EACH BREATH
THE UNIVERSE
SPEAKS TO US
SLOWLY
GENTLY
CONNECTING EVERY MOMENT
AS IT WAS AND AS IT WILL BE
FROM THE BEGINNING THROUGH TO
ALL ETERNITY

I CHOOSE TO LET THE LIGHT SHINE

"Life isn't about finding yourself, it's about creating yourself."
– George Bernard Shaw

journey

TAKE A
step
YOUR LIFE'S
Path
SUMMONS

THINGS WILL NEVER BE THE SAME
THERE WILL NEVER BE ANY REGRETS
IF I HAD IT ALL TO DO AGAIN
I WOULD

NIGHT DISINTEGRATES
SUNSET SETS THE SKY ON FIRE
WHITE HORIZONS WAIT

"As long as we are creating, we are cultivating meaning." –
Brene Brown

LOVE

I WANT TO
Capture EVERY moment
MAKE it A MEMORY
etched in Eternity
TO ReCALL
when the moment
HAS PASSED
CAPTURE YOUR SMILE
CAPTURE YOUR VOICE
CAPTURE YOUR HUGS

IT IS NOT
WHO DO YOU
THINK
YOU ARE

IT IS WHO DOES
your heart
FEEL
YOU TO BE

HOLD ONTO THE SOUND
VIBRATING IN YOUR HEART
WAITING TO FIND ITS WAY
INTO A WORLD
HUNGRY FOR WORDS
SPOKEN IN SILENCES

“Writing is the painting of the voice.” – Voltaire

RELAX
RELAX
RELAX
RELAX
RELAX
RELAX
RELAX
RELAX

I AM
where
I NEED TO BE
IF I WAS NOT
I WOULD NOT
be
here

Speak the
LANGUAGE
OF TREES
Whispered
IN THE BREEZE
PUTTING
your
MIND
AT
EASE

There is art in heART
Put your heart in your art
Feel it!

“Art washes from the soul the dust of everyday life.”
– Pablo Picasso

Shine
BOO

In the stillness
We must face ourselves
And be comfortable
In our own silence

ACCEPT WHO YOU ARE
WORTHY OF THE LIGHT
IMPRINTED WITH THE ECHOS OF STARS

connect
TO
SUNSHINE

Quotes used in this book that are excerpts from the following published poems:

Ksiezopolski, Susan, (2014),Writing for Change, Canada, My Words Press
They Came, pg. 113
Lilies, pg. 30
Clematis, pg. 31
Summer, pg. 37
Search of sleep, pg. 53
Truth speaks, pg. 61
The ancients, pg. 73
Capture every moment, pg.74
Take a Step, pg. 94
They Came, pg.112

Ksiezopolski, Susan, (2012), My Words, Canada, My Words Press
What Is, pg. 206
Serenity, pg. 195
Busyness of Life, pg. 216
I'm Here, pg. 228
Resonance of the Universe, pg. 247
Things, pg.294
Timeless Friendship, pg. 295
The irony of Life, 338
Who do you Think You Are, pg.350
More Snippets, pg. 384
Making Meaning, 385

Quotes used in this book that are excerpts from the following published poems (Cont.):

My Words Facebook
www.facebook.com/mywordsfrommyheart/

About Miracles
Heart Song
Creative Energy
Healing Song
Horizons
Paradox of Eternity
Run your Race
Shadows
Shine
Summer Rain
Trees
Users Guide

Acknowledgements

We would like to express our deepest gratitude to Visual Arts Mississauga (VAM) and the Mississauga Arts Council (MAC), the catalysts and art champions that were instrumental in bringing us together which resulted in the collaboration to create this book.

Annis Karpenko, Executive Director of VAM set the stage for us to first meet. Mike Douglas, Executive Director of Mississauga Arts Councils' vision to support local artists by implementing micogrants, presented us with the opportunity to brain storm and come up with ideas to create new art. Being awarded the 2019 MAC Fusion Grant lit the spark behind "Fuel Your Creativity".

We would like to also thank our families for their input into each step along the way of designing, laying out, creating and reviewing the content and the final outcome. Their encouragement and support are the energy that sustain us and empower us to create.

We also acknowledge the magically mysterious force of the Universe/God that has guided us to find each other, and has since opened doors to clear the path for this book to find its way to you.

We are grateful that you have been drawn to this book. May it become a tool to fuel your creativity and unleashing your own inner brilliance.

"Inspiration exists, but it has to find you working."
– Pablo Picasso

About the Author

Poetry speaks softly, heard through the dialogue of inspiring words weaving stories. Through the rhythm and rhyme of verse on the page, the dialogue of self is heard. Narratives conveying experiences of the human condition are composed and shared shattering isolation, connecting us. Writing is the oxygen fuelling self-expression, unleashing the power to transform.

"Through writing, I can exhale and express what I take in, in life." – Susan Ksiezopolski

To find out more about Susan's poetry visit:
www.mywordsnow.com

About the Illustrator

Art speaks in bold colours and vivid textures. Each brush stroke makes a statement, illustrating and liberating all thoughts and feelings. Mindless doodles arise from the canvas, expressing emotions emerging from reflections within. Outpourings of images awaken wonder, silencing the mindless chatter as impressions surface and connect the art to meaning.

"*When I paint my subconscious self is speaking what I can not express in words"* – Angela Chao

To find out more about Angela's art visit:
www.mindlessdoodle.ca

For more about Susan and Angela's collaborative work visit www.createconvergence.com or you can contact them at info@createconvergence.com